SANDY

COMPLETE RECORDI

ANDREW S.

With afterword by Ian Meacheam

Essential Discographies No.28

APS Publications
Yorkshire

APS Publications

www.andrewsparke.com

ISBN 9781789960686

NOTES

This short book simply collects the recorded work of Sandy Denny, arguably the true female voice of the English folk revival and its aim is simply to save record buyers hours of research online while giving them a presentation catalogue for the bookshelf.

www.sandydennyofficial.com

.

COMPILER'S NOTE

Looking back it sometimes feels that there at least three different versions of Sandy Denny, if not more, each of them overlapping but conflicting and only her awesome talent uniting them into anything which might pass as a single entity.

The Sandy Denny I knew first was woman who was such a vital part of Fairport Convention. Although not their original singer, it was she who did so much to steer their transition into a blend of folk and rock which was entirely knew and yet organically rooted in the English tradition.

As a solo singer, Sandy Denny grew into something different, moving effortlessly between the worlds of folk and the role of femme fatale torch singer. She even tackled and made her own such an iconic song as Elton John's *Candle In The Wind*. A unique singer, she brought all manner of unusual phrasings and tones to all the material she chose to record. Nobody ever sounded like her then or since.

Naturally enough her early career as a soloist represent a younger, more tentative version of Sandy Denny but even then a strength of delivery is apparent even where the songs didn't coalesce into a unified portfolio.

Lastly there was the haunted element of Sandy Denny: the insecurities, the dependence on alcohol, the relationship issues which sit so strangely alongside the headstrong confidence of the woman who was always clearly Robert Plant's equal duetting on *The Battle Of Evermore* for Led Zeppelin's *Four Symbols* album.

How can anyone make sense of all these contradictions? Perhaps nobody ever could although several biographers have tried with greater or lesser degrees of success. She was a tragedy. She was a triumph. She was a lost soul. She was music. All such judgments have a strong element of truth in them but Sandy Denny remains elusive.

I can only reconcile the sense that she was taken too early when she died of a brain haemorrhage by taking down a copy of my favourite of all her works, 'The North Star Grassman and The Ravens'. As the first sad notes of *Late November* spill out the years drop away and I'm transported back down the years. I'm one of three teenagers in my friend John Phillips's room again, two of us on the bed and one on the floor, his back against the wall - John puts his newly purchased album on the record deck and places the stylus carefully in the first groove. And it's the shock of an immediate recognition in the unfamiliar Intro and a gleeful endorsement of another record to join an exclusive band of lifelong favourites. I can remember holding the gatefold cardboard sleeve in my hands and wondering why Island Records product even smelled different. And that music full of longing and of place, somehow promising that all would be right with the world.

And that's what Sandy Denny's music does – it makes everything over anew and there can be no greater gift from a musician than that.

Andrew Sparke

Sandy Denny with Fotheringay

SANDY DENNY

Initially a young walk in singer at various folk clubs, a young Sandy Denny made her first 1960s recordings with the likes of Alex Campbell and Johnny Silvio. She was 21 when she achieved her breakthrough in 1968, replacing singer Judy Dyble in Fairport Convention, with Denny to become the prime exponents of a new English musical revolution mixing folk music with a rock rhythm section and electric guitars. Over the first 18 months of a mere ten year career in the limelight, Denny and her bandmates cut three of the quintessential albums of the era culminating in 'Liege And Lief' which set the standards by which all such fusions are judged to this day.

Denny quit the Fairports in 1969 and used the next four years to create her own band, Fotheringay, to indulge in rock 'n' roll mayhem as The Bunch and to record three superb solo albums. She also made her own unique vocal contributions to Led Zeppelin's fourth album.

Denny rejoined Fairport Convention from 1973-1976, a period in which the band toured extensively (hence the belated release of several concert records from the period) and made the 'Rising For the Moon' album. However unbeknown to anyone time was running out for Denny and after leaving the band for a second time she made only one more solo album before she was taken cruelly young by a brain haemorrhage following a fall at a friend's house.

The obvious question which falls to be asked is what she might have done musically had she lived the lifespan she might have expected to be granted?

EARLY RECORDS

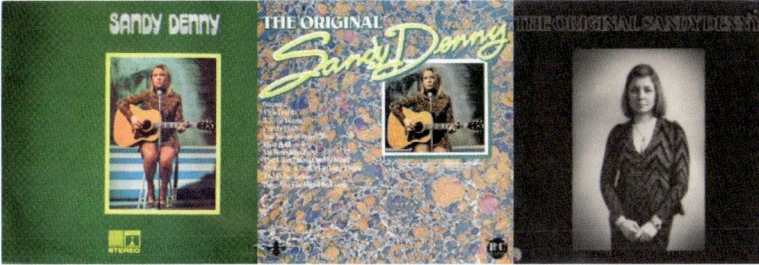

IT'S SANDY DENNY *(Saga 1970)*

This Train
The 3.10 to Yuma
Pretty Polly
You Never Wanted Me
Milk and Honey
My Ramblin' Boy

The Last Thing on My Mind
Make Me a Pallet On Your
Floor
The False Bride
Been on the Road So Long

*Songs **Sandy Denny** recorded for Saga Records in 1967, initially released on two separate albums: 'Alex Campbell and his Friends' and '**Sandy** and Johnny'. The album was reissued (Mooncrest 1978) as 'The Original Sandy Denny' and again as 'Where the Time Goes - Sandy '67' (Castle 2005) an album which includes 5 alternate takes. The album has also been released elsewhere simply as 'Sandy Denny'.*

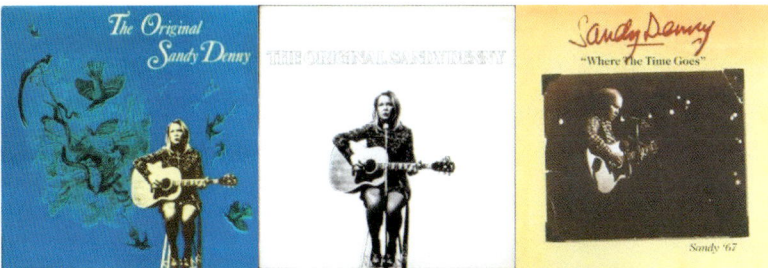

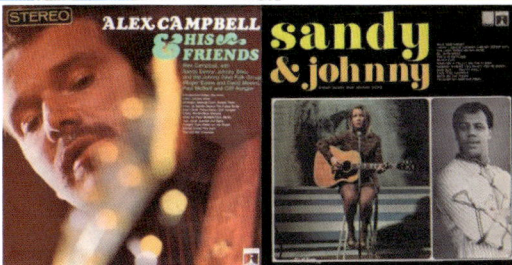

SOLO ALBUMS

THE NORTH STAR GRASSMAN AND THE RAVENS *(Island 1971)*

Late November
Blackwaterside
The Sea Captain
Down In The Flood
John The Gun
Next Time Around
The Optimist
Let's Jump The Broomstick
Wretched Wilbur
The North Star Grassman And The Ravens
Crazy Lady Blues

SANDY *(Island 1972)*

It'll Take a Long Time
Sweet Rosemary
For Nobody to Hear
Tomorrow Is a Long Time
Quiet Joys of Brotherhood
Listen, Listen
The Lady
Bushes and Briars
It Suits Me Well
The Music Weaver

2012 CD reissue includes previously unreleased concert 'Live at Ebbetts Field'

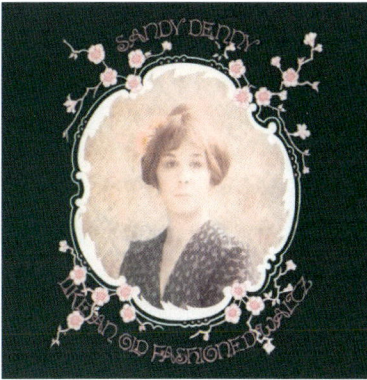

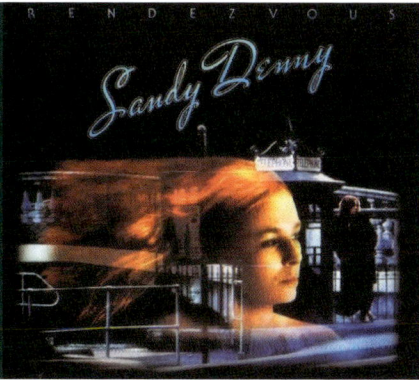

LIKE AN OLD FASHIONED WALTZ
(Island 1973)

Solo
Like an Old Fashioned Waltz
Whispering Grass
Friends
Carnival
Dark the Night
At the End of the Day
Until the Real Thing Comes Along
No End

RENDEZVOUS
(Island 1977)

I Wish I Was a Fool for You (For Shame of Doing Wrong)
Gold Dust
Candle in the Wind
Take Me Away
One Way Donkey Ride
I'm a Dreamer
All Our Days
Silver Threads and Golden Needles
No More Sad Refrains

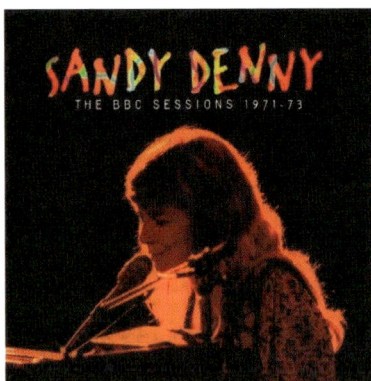

THE BBC SESSIONS 1971-1973
(Strange Fruit 1997)

Northstar Grassman

Sweet Rosemary

The Lady

Next Time Around

Blackwaterside

John The Gun

Late November

The Optimist

Crazy Lady Blues

The Lowlands Of Holland

It Suits Me Well

Bushes And Briars

The Music Weaver

It'll Take A Long Time

Who Knows Where The Time Goes?

Until The Real Thing Comes Along

Whispering Grass

Like An Old Fashioned Waltz

Dark The Night

Solo

Rare album – only 3500 copies before withdrawn from sale due to copyright issues. Material has since been made available on LIVE AT THE BBC

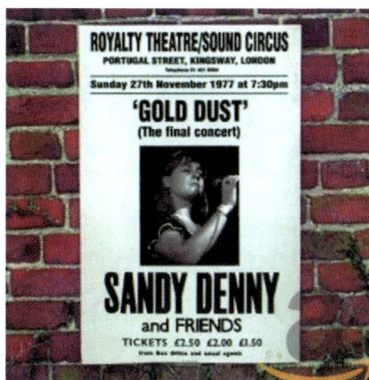

GOLD DUST
(Island 1998)

I Wish I Was A Fool For You
Stranger To Himself
I'm A Dreamer
Take Me Away
Nothing More
The Sea
The Lady
Gold Dust
Solo
John The Gun
It'll Take A Long Time
Wretched Wilbur
Tomorrow Is A Long Time
The North Star Grassman
One More Chance
No More Sad Refrains
Who Knows Where The Time Goes

Live from Denny's final tour in 1977 but with new backing track to resolve instrumental issues on the night. Also changed running order when reviewed against bootleg recording of same concert.

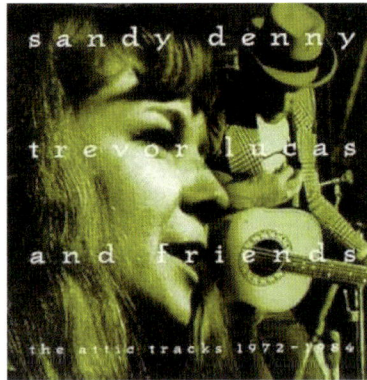

THE ATTIC TRACKS 1972-1985
(Raven Records 1995)

Moments
The Ballad of Ned Kelly (live)
Ecoute, Ecoute
One More Chance (home demo)
Rising for the Moon (home demo)
Tears
Easy to Slip
Losing Game
Girls on the Avenue
Breakaway
Still Waters Run Deep
The King and Queen of England (home demo)
No End (solo piano version)
The Town I Loved So Well (live)
Forever Young (live)
Gold Dust (live)
Stranger to Himself (live)
Who Knows Where the Times Goes? (live)

Compilation drawn from four cassette only releases by Friends Of Fairport Convention.

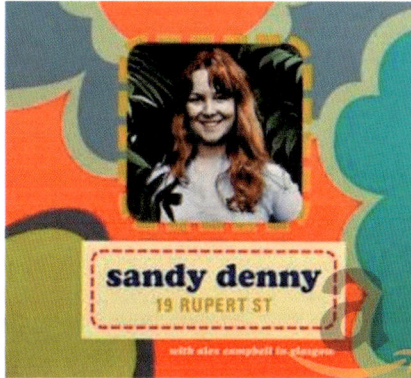

19 RUPERT STREET
(Witchwood 2011)

The Leaves Of Life
Willie Moore
Balulalow
The Sans Day Carol
Trouble In Mind
Jimmie Brown The Newsboy
The Midnight Special
Milk And Honey
Who Knows Where The Time Goes
Fairy Tale Lullaby
She Moves Through The Fair
Chuffa Chuff Chuff/Clementine/Jesus Loves Me

SINGLES

Crazy Lady Blues/Let's Jump The Broomstick *(A&M 1971)*

Listen Listen/Tomorrow Is A Long Time *(Island 1972)*

Late November/Let's Jump The Broomstick *(Island 1972)*

Whispering Grass/Friends *(Island 1973)*

Like An Old Fashioned Waltz/John The Gun *(Island 1975)*

Candle In The Wind/Still Waters Run Deep *(Island 1977)*

Make Me A Pallet On Your Floor/Train *(Mooncrest 1978)*

She Moves Through The Fair/Geordie/Boxful Of Treasures/They
Don't Seem To Know You/Go Your Way My Love
(Stamford Audio 2007)

I'm A Dreamer/Who Knows Where The Time Goes? *(Universal 2011)*

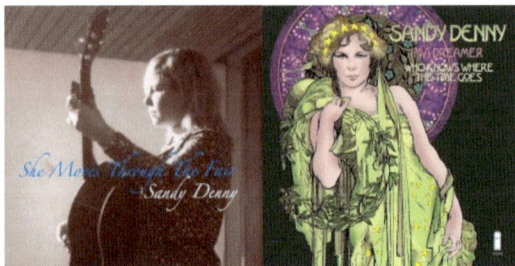

OTHER APPEARANCES

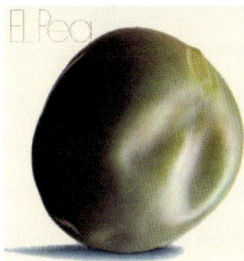

EL PEA *(Island 1971)*

Compilation album featuring alternative version of 'Late November' to the one which appeared on 'The Northstar Grassman And The Ravens' (but which has since appeared on the re-mastered CD of The Northstar Grassman and the Ravens and the 'Sandy Denny' box set).

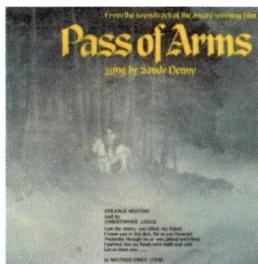

Pass Of Arms *(Island 1972)*

Seven inch single which formed the soundtrack to a short film by Peter Elford. The soundtrack was provided by Don Fraser and featured two songs performed by Sandy Denny (plus a recitation by Christopher Logue of the poem 'Strange Meeting' by Wilfred Owen). Both the Sandy Denny tracks are available on the anthology 'No More Sad Refrains' and as bonus tracks on the 2005 CD reissue of 'Sandy'.

Here In Silence
Man Of Iron

BOX SETS

A BOXFUL OF TREASURES *(Fledg'ling Records 2004)*

The 3:10 To Yuma
She Moves Through The Fair *(home recording)*
Boxful Of Treasures *(home recording)*
They Don't Seem to Know You *(home recording)*
Go Your Way My Love *(home recording)*
Geordie *(home recording)*
Been On The Road So Long
You Never Wanted Me *(Alex Campbell & Friends)*
This Train *(Alex Campbell & Friends)*
Sail Away To The Sea *(Sandy Denny and Strawbs)*
Tell Me What You See In Me *(Sandy Denny and Strawbs)*
Who Knows Where The Time Goes? *(Sandy Denny and Strawbs)*
Autopsy *(demo)*
Now And Then
I Don't Know Where I Stand *(Fairport Convention - radio session)*
Bird on a Wire *(Fairport Convention - radio session)*
Fotheringay *(Fairport Convention)*
Nottamun Town *(Fairport Convention)*
Meet On The Ledge *(Fairport Convention)*

Si tu dois partir *(Fairport Convention)*
Cajun Woman *(Fairport Convention)*
The Ballad Of Easy Rider *(Fairport Convention)*
A Sailor's Life *(Fairport Convention)*
Reynardine *(Fairport Convention)*
Farewell, Farewell *(Fairport Convention)*
Tam Lin *(Fairport Convention)*
Sir Patrick Spens *(radio session)*
The Pond And The Stream *(Fotheringay)*
The Sea *(Fotheringay)*
Banks Of The Nile *(Fotheringay)*
Silver Threads and Golden Needles *(Fotheringay)*
The Lowlands of Holland *(radio session)*
Nothing More *(Fotheringay)*
Gypsy Davey *(Fotheringay)*
Late November *(Fotheringay)*
Northstar Grassman and The Ravens
Next Time Around *(alternate take without strings)*
Blackwaterside
The Sea Captain
Thru My Eyes *(Ian Matthews)*
Learning The Game (The Bunch)
Here In Silence
Bruton Town (radio session)
Sweet Rosemary (demo)
After Halloween (demo)
The Lady (demo)
The Music Weaver
Ecoute Ecoute
Quiet Joys Of Brotherhood
It'll Take A Long Time
No End *(solo alternate take)*
Bushes and Briars *(radio session)*
Walking The Floor Over You
Whispering Grass *(radio session)*
Solo
At the End of the Day *(alternate take without strings)*

Like An Old Fashioned Waltz
Until The Real Thing Comes Along *(radio session)*
John The Gun *(live - Fairport Convention)*
She Moves Through The Fair *(live – Fairport Convention)*
One More Chance *(demo version)*
The King And Queen Of England *(home recording)*
Rising For The Moon *(Fairport Convention)*
White Dress *(Fairport Convention)*
I'm A Dreamer
By The Time It Gets Dark *(previously unreleased)*
No More Sad Refrains
Losing Game *(previously unreleased)*
Easy To Slip
Full Moon
Moments *(final studio recording)*
One Way Donkey Ride *(previously unreleased)*
I'm A Dreamer *(previously unreleased)*
Take Me Away *(previously unreleased)*
Rising For The Moon *(previously unreleased)*
Still Waters Run Deep *(previously unreleased)*
All Our Days *(previously unreleased)*
No More Sad Refrains *(previously unreleased)*
By The Time It Gets Dark *(previously unreleased)*
The Music Weaver *(demo)*
What Is True? *(demo)*
Stranger To Himself *(demo)*
Take Away The Load *(demo)*
By The Time It Gets Dark *(previously unreleased)*
Full Moon *(demo)*
Knockin' on Heaven's Door *(live)*
It'll Take A Long Time *(previously unreleased)*
Who Knows Where the Time Goes? *(live)*

5 CD deluxe box set. Including previously unreleased outtake, demos and alternate versions as well as a whole disc of home recordings.

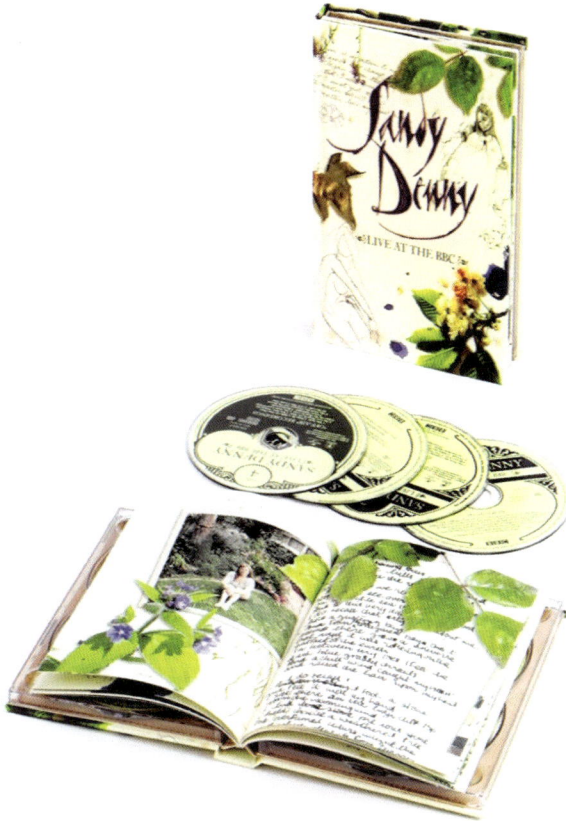

LIVE AT THE BBC
(Island 2007)

Fhir a' Bhata (The Boatmen)
Green Grow the Laurels
Hold on to Me Babe
Blues Run the Game
Late November
The Optimist
Crazy Lady Blues
The Lowlands of Holland
It Suits Me Well
The Music Weaver
Bushes and Briars
It'll Take a Long Time
Solo

Like an Old Fashioned Waltz
Who Knows Where the Time Goes?
Until the Real Thing Comes Along
Whispering Grass
Dark the Night
Solo
The North Star Grassman and the Ravens
Sweet Rosemary
The Lady
Bruton Town
Next Time Around
Blackwaterside
John the Gun
The Lady
Bushes and Briars
It Suits Me Well
Blackwaterside
The Music Weaver
The Sea Captain
John the Gun
Interview
The North Star Grassman and the Ravens
Crazy Lady Blues
Late November
This Train
Make Me a Pallet on Your Floor
The Last Thing on My Mind
You Never Wanted Me
Been on the Road So Long
The Quiet Land of Erin
Sweet Nightingale (duet with Mick Groves)
Blackwaterside
The North Star Grassman and the Ravens
The Lady
It'll Take a Long Time
4 CD box set

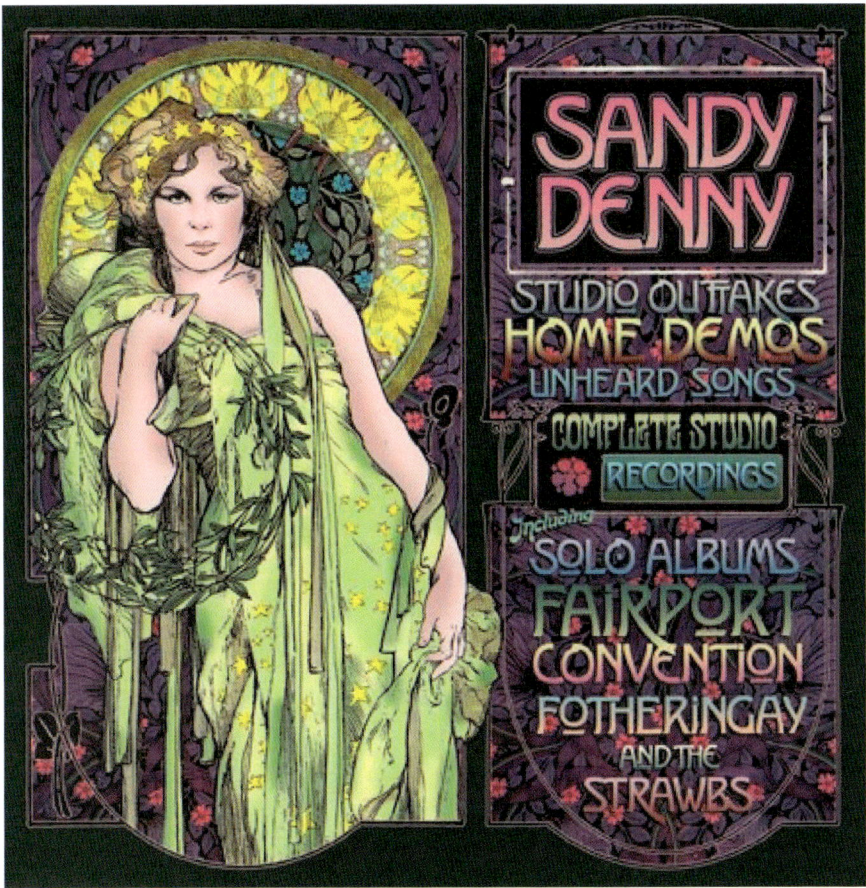

SANDY DENNY
(Universal/Island 2010)

Lavishly beautiful limited edition 19-CD box set - 11 CDs are dedicated to Sandy Denny's complete commercial recordings with Alex Campbell, Johnny Silvo, Fotheringay, Strawbs, Fairport Convention and solo all with bonus material in the form of outtakes, demos and live recordings - 8 further CDs contain unreleased song, demos, unreleased BBC recordings, alternate takes, live recordings, acoustic versions, and rare radio interviews. The set includes 103 unreleased versions of Sandy Denny's recordings (64 studio takes, 25 demos and 14 live recordings). The set includes rare print items such as a hardback book containing rare photos, a reproduction of a notebook containing handwritten lyrics. And a copy of an original Island press kit.

The Sandy Denny boxed set subsequently spawned a 4 CD sampler containing 75 tracks, including 17 demos, rarities and alternate versions.

THE NOTES AND THE WORDS: A COLLECTION OF DEMOS AND RARITIES *(Universal/Island 2012)*

The Early Home Demos
Blues Run The Game
Soho
It Ain't Me Babe
East Virginia
Geordie
In Memory (The Tender Years)
I Love My True Love
Ethusel
Carnival
They Don't Seem To Know You
Gerrard Street
Seven Virgins
A Little Bit Of Rain
Go Your Own Way My Love
Cradle Song
Who Knows Where The Time Goes
Motherless Children
Alex Campbell And His Friends
You Never Wanted Me
Milk And Honey
Sandy Denny Solo
She Moves Through The Fair
Fotheringay
Now And Then
Autopsy
Swedish Fly Girls (Film Soundtrack)

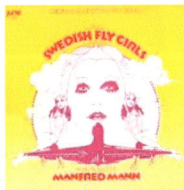

Are The Judges Sane
Fairport Convention
Mr. Lacey
The Ballad Of Easy Rider
A Sailor's Life
Come All Ye
Matty Groves
Fotheringay
The Way I Feel
The Sea
Winter Winds
The Pond And The Stream
Fotheringay
John The Gun
The North Star Grassman And The Ravens
Late November
Next Time Around
Lord Bateman
The Optimist
Wretched Wilbur
Crazy Lady Blues
North Star Grassman And The Ravens
Blackwaterside
Sandy
It'll Take A Long Time
For Nobody To Hear
Quiet Joys Of Brotherhood
The Lady
Bushes And Briars
The Music Weaver
No End
Like An Old Fashioned Waltz
Solo

Whispering Grass
Friends
Dark The Night
Until The Real Thing Comes
Along
Home Demos
The King And Queen Of
England
After Halloween
Take Away The Load
Stranger To Himself
By The Time It Gets Dark
Fairport Convention Live At The L.A.
Troubadour 1974
Down In The Flood
Knocking On Heaven's Door
Like An Old Fashioned Waltz

Fairport Convention Rising For The
Moon
Dawn
One More Chance
What Is True?
Rendezvous
No More Sad Refrains
I Wish I Was A Fool For You
Gold Dust
Candle In The Wind
One Way Donkey Ride
I'm A Dreamer
Still Waters Run Deep
Full Moon
Moments
Makes Me Think Of You

COMPILATIONS

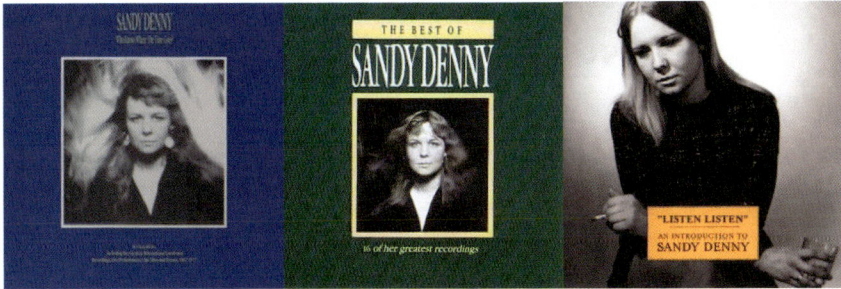

WHO KNOWS WHERE THE TIME GOES? *(Island 1985)*
THE BEST OF SANDY DENNY *(Island 1987)*
LISTEN, LISTEN *(Island 1999)*

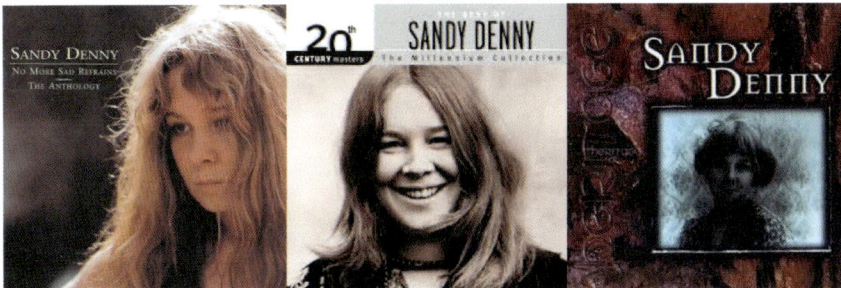

NO MORE SAD REFRAINS: THE ANTHOLOGY *(A&M 2000)*
THE BEST OF SANDY DENNY *(A&M 2002)*
HERITAGE *(Disky 2003)*

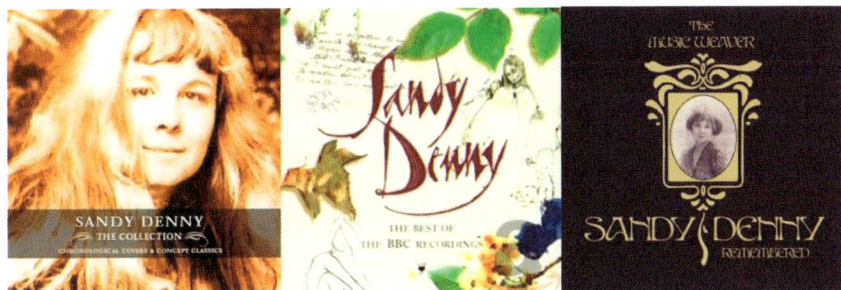

THE COLLECTION *(Spectrum 2004)*
THE BEST OF THE BBC RECORDINGS *(Island 2008)*
THE MUSIC WEAVER *(Island 2008)*

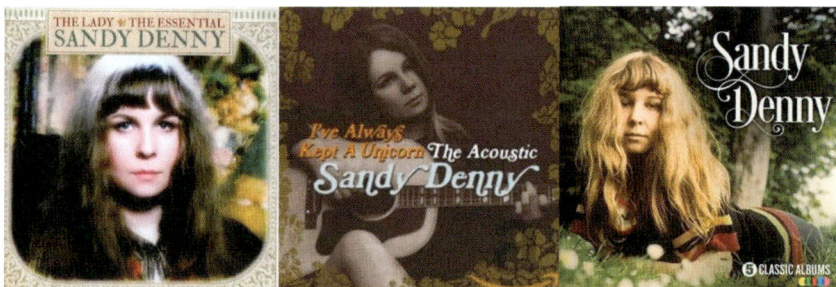

THE LADY: THE ESSENTIAL SANDY DENNY *(Spectrum 2013)*
I'VE ALWAYS KEPT A UNICORN: THE ACOUSTIC SANDY DENNY
(Spectrum 2016)
FIVE CLASSIC ALBUMS *(Spectrum 2016)*

SANDY DENNY WITH THE STRAWBS

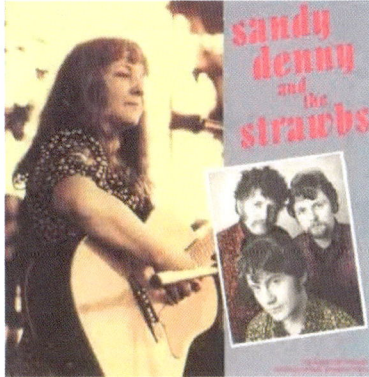

ALL OUR OWN WORK *(Hallmark 1973)*

On My Way
Who Knows Where The Time Goes
Tell Me What You See In Me
Always On My Mind
Stay Awhile With Me
Wild Strawberries
All I Need Is You
How Everyone But Sam Was A Hypocrite
Sail Away To The Sea
Sweetling
Nothing Else Will Do Babe
And You Need Me

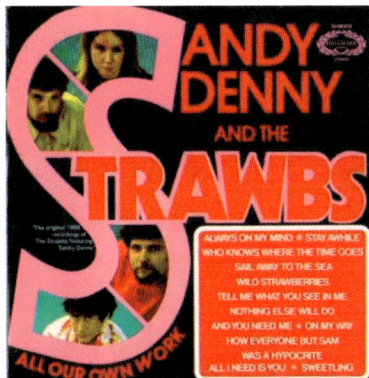

Poor Jimmy Wilson
I've Been My Own Worst Friend
Two Weeks Last Summer

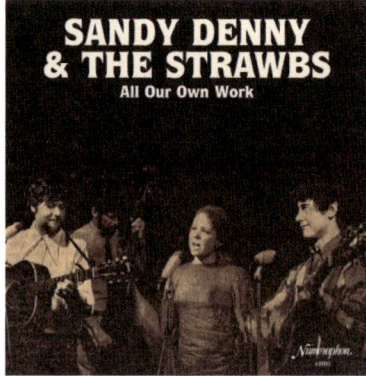

2014 Numerophon vinyl reissue adds out-takes to original 12 track album
Two Weeks Last Summer
Who Knows Where The Time Goes
Tell Me What You See In Me
Stay Awhile With Me
Nothing Else Will Do Babe
And You Need Me
I've Been My Own Worst Friend
Poor Jimmy Wilson
Strawberry Picking
Pieces Of 79 And 15
The Falling Leaves
Indian Summer

FAIRPORT CONVENTION

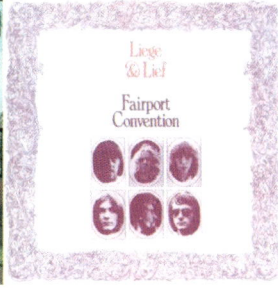

WHAT WE DID ON OUR HOLIDAYS
(Island 1969)

Fotheringay
Mr. Lacey
Book Song
The Lord Is In This Place
No Man's Land
I'll Keep It With Mine

Eastern Rain
Nottamun Town
Tale In Hard Time
She Moves Through The Fair
Meet On The Ledge
End Of A Holiday

UNHALFBRICKING
(Island 1969)

Genesis Hall
Si Tu Dois Partir
Autopsy
A Sailor's Life
Cajun Woman

Who Knows Where The Time
Goes?
Percy's Song
Million Dollar Bash

LIEGE AND LIEF
(Island 1969)

Come All Ye
Reynardine
Matty Groves
Farewell, Farewell
The Deserter

Medley: The Lark In The
Morning
Tam Lin
Crazy Man Michael

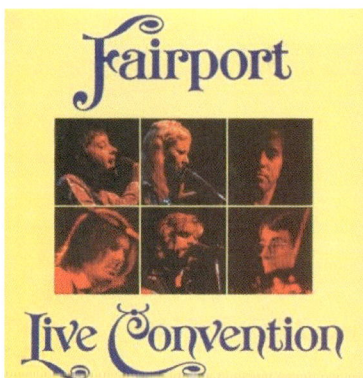

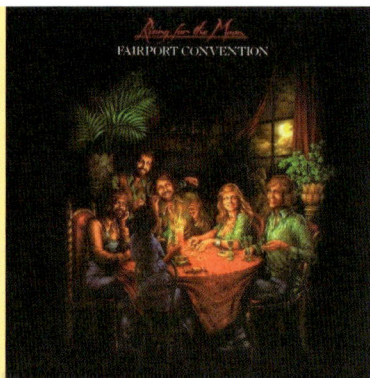

FAIRPORT LIVE CONVENTION
(Island 1974)

Matty Groves
Rosie
Fiddlestix
John The Gun
Something You Got

Sloth
Dirty Linen
Down In The Flood
John B. MacKenzie

RISING FOR THE MOON
(Island 1975)

Rising for the Moon
Restless
White Dress
Let It Go
Stranger To Himself
What Is True?
Iron Lion
Dawn

After Hallowe'en
Night-Time Girl
One More Chance
2005 CD reissue adds:
Tears
Rising For The Moon (demo)
Stranger To Himself (demo)
One More Chance (demo)

*The above Fairport Convention titles cover all the official releases and recording made in the two spells when Sandy Denny was a member of the band. For absolute completeness it's worth noting that in recent years as copyrights and licences have expired or been transferred between companies a large number of new live Fairport albums have materialised, several containing contributions from Denny. Whether they are worth collecting for those contributions is a matter of individual taste but if you lean towards obsessive end of the collecting spectrum please consult the sister title to this book published contemporaneously **Fairport Convention: Complete Recordings Illustrated**.*

THE BUNCH

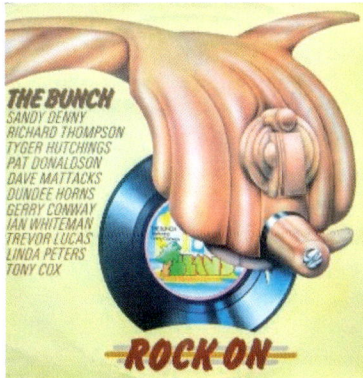

THE BUNCH
(Island 1972)

Crazy Arms
That'll Be The Day
Don't Be Cruel
The Loco-Motion
My Girl In The Month Of May
Love's Made A Fool Of You
Willie And The Hand Jive
Jambalaya (On The Bayou)
When Will I Be Loved
Nadine
Sweet Little Rock 'N' Roller
Learning The Game

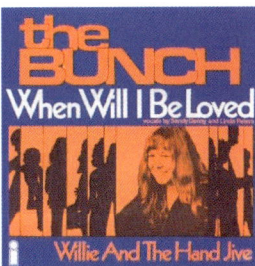

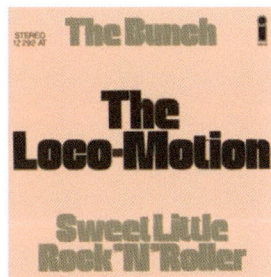

SINGLES

When Will I Be Loved/ Willie And The Hand Jive *(Island 1972)*
The Loco-Motion/Sweet Little Rock 'N' Roller *(Island 1972)*

FOTHERINGAY

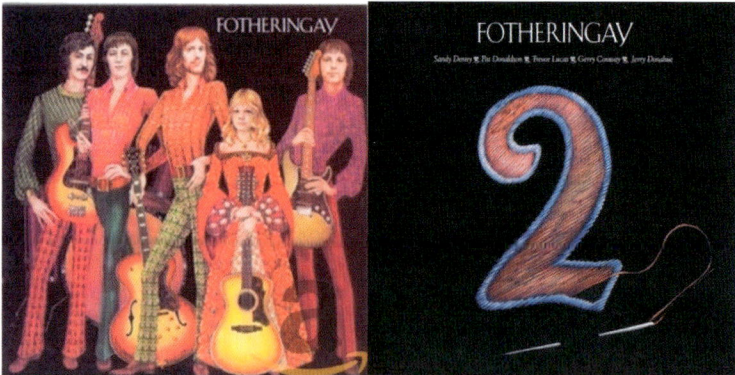

FOTHERINGAY *(Island 1970)*

Nothing More
The Sea
The Ballad of Ned Kelly
Winter Winds
Peace in the End
The Way I Feel
The Pond and the Stream
Too Much of Nothing
Banks of the Nile

FOTHERINGAY 2 *(Fled'ling Records 2006)*

John the Gun
Eppie Moray
Wild Mountain Thyme
Knights of the Road
Late November
Restless
Gypsy Davey
I Don't Believe You
Silver Threads and Golden Needles
Bold Jack Donahue
Two Weeks Last Summer

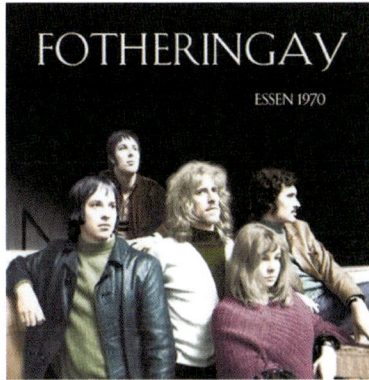

ESSEN 1970

Eppie Moray
The Sea
The Ballad of Ned Kelly
Gypsy Davey
Too Much of Nothing

Nothing More
The Way I Feel
John the Gun
Memphis Tennessee

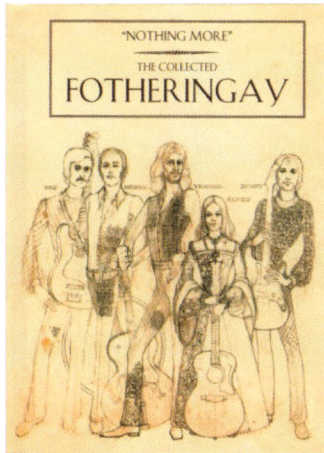

NOTHING MORE (THE COLLECTED FOTHERINGAY) *(Island 2015)*

Complete Fotheringay and Fotheringay 2 albums plus bonus and live recordings:
The Sea (studio demo)
Winter Winds (studio demo)
The Pond And The Stream (studio demo)
The Way I Feel (original version)
Banks Of The Nile (alternate take)

Late November (Joe Boyd mix)
Gypsey Dave (Joe Boyd mix)
Two Weeks Last Summer (Joe Boyd mix)
Silver Threads And Golden Needles (2004 version)
Bruton Town (rehearsal)
Bruton Town (2015 version)
Live In Rotterdam 1970
The Way I Feel
The Sea
Too Much of Nothing
Nothing More
Winter
I'm Troubled
Two Weeks Last Summer
The Ballad Of Ned Kelly
Banks of the Nile
Memphis Tennessee
BBC live recordings 1979
Interview/The Sea
The Lowlands Of Holland
Eppie Moray
John The Gun

SINGLES

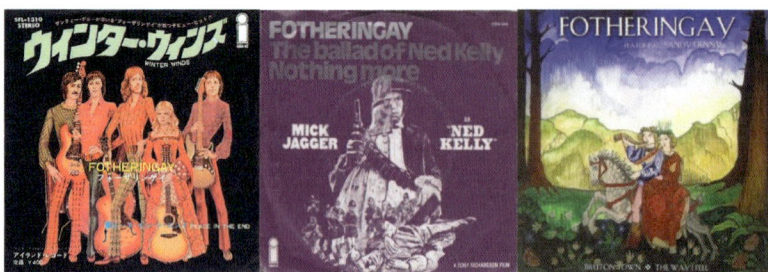

Winter Winds/Peace In The End *(Island 1970)*
The Way I Feel/The Way I Feel *(A&M 1970)*
Peace In The End/Winter Winds *(Island 1970)*
The Ballad Of Ned Kelly/Nothing More *(Island 1971)*
Bruton Town/ The Way I Feel *(Island 2015)*

DVDs

FURTHER READING

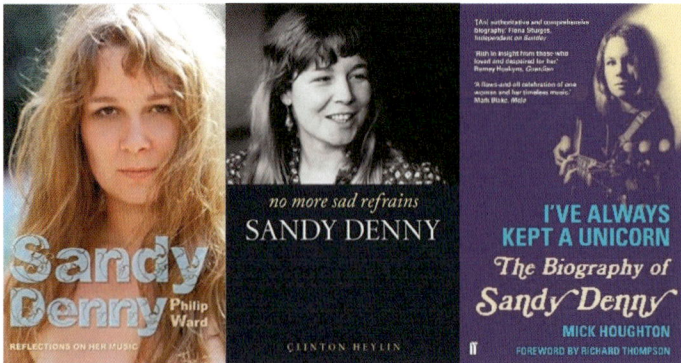

AFTERWORD
IAN MEACHEAM

In late March 1978, while on holiday with her parents and her baby Georgia in Cornwall, Mrs Lucas was injured when she fell down a staircase and hit her head on concrete. Following the incident, she suffered from intense headaches. A doctor prescribed her a powerful painkiller which can have serious side effects when mixed with alcohol.

At some unknown point during the first half of April 1978, Alexandra Lucas suffered yet another major fall at her home. On 13th April, concerned about Alexandra's erratic behaviour and fearing for his daughter's safety, her husband, Mr Trevor Lucas, left the family home without telling her and returned to his native Australia with their child.

On discovering Lucas's departure, Alexandra went to stay at the home of her friend Miranda Ward. During this time, she apparently made an appointment to speak with a doctor about her headaches, and also intended to get advice about her alcohol addiction. On 17th April, the day of the doctor's appointment and while Ms Ward was at work, another acquaintance found Mrs Lucas unconscious at the foot of the staircase which led to the second floor of the house. She was rushed by ambulance to Queen Mary's Hospital in Roehampton.

On 19 April, she was transferred to Atkinson Morley Hospital in Wimbledon. After receiving the news that Mrs Lucas was in a coma, her husband returned from Australia. Upon his arrival at the hospital, doctors informed him that his wife was effectively brain-dead and her condition would not improve. Mr Lucas accepted their recommendation to turn off the life-support machines. Mrs Lucas was pronounced dead at 7:50 pm on 21st April 1978. At the inquest her death was ruled to be the result of a traumatic mid-brain haemorrhage and blunt force trauma to her head.

She was thirty-one years old.

ESSENTIAL DISCOGRAPHIES FROM APS BOOKS
(www.andrewsparke.com)

Abba Alan Parsons Project Alan Stivell Alex Harvey Alice Cooper
Amon Duul II Amy Winehouse Andy White Bangles
Barclay James Harvest Blockheads Blondie Blue Nile Bo Hansson
Bonzo Dog Band Bruce Cockburn Can Caravan Catherine Howe Cher
Clifford T.Ward Colin Blunstone Culture Curved Air Doors Ekseption
Emerson Lake & Palmer Enid Fad Gadget Fagans Fairport Convention
Faust Fish Focus Frankie Miller Gaslight Anthem Gavin DeGraw
Gentle Giant George Michael Gil Scott-Heron Graham Parker
Groundhogs Ian Dury Ian Hunter Ijahman James McMurtry Jeff Beck
Jess Roden Jethro Tull Joan Armatrading John Lennon John Martyn
John Prine John Stewart Johnny Clegg Kate Bush Kevin Ayers Kinks
Kraftwerk Led Zeppelin Leonard Cohen Linda Ronstadt Luka Bloom
Lyle Lovett Lynyrd Skynyrd Madison Violet Marillion Meal Ticket
Michael Chapman Mike Oldfield Monkees Nick Drake Osibisa Patricia
Kaas Paul Kelly Pavlov's Dog Pink Floyd Pretenders Pretty Things
Procol Harum Richard Thompson Rory Gallagher Rumer Sandy Denny
Savoy Brown Show Of Hands Starry Eyed and Laughing Steeleye Span
Steely Dan Steve Gibbons Steve Hackett Sting Stomu Yamash'ta
Stone The Crows Strawbs Supertramp 10cc Tom Robinson Tom Waits
Tori Amos Troggs Waking The Witch Warren Zevon Willie Nile
Wishbone Ash Xray Spex ZZ Top

APS PUBLICATIONS

Printed in Great Britain
by Amazon